# The Invitation
## and Five Other Dramas
## for Tweens

**Abingdon Press**
Nashville

The Invitation
and Five Other Dramas for Tweens

ISBN: 978-0-687-64713-2

# Written by Nate Lee

Cover design by Keitha Vincent

08 09 10 11 12 13 14 15 16 17—10 9 8 7 6 5 4 3 2 1

Manufactured in the United States of America

# Contents

# The Invitation

## Production Notes
*This is a modern version of the parable of the great banquet,*
*Luke 14:15-24. The dress and the situations are modern.*

## Characters

### Speaking Roles
Butler (Edmond)
Old Man
Albert
Brenda
Carrie
Dave
Ellen
Fred

## Props

*high-backed, expensive-looking chair*
*desk*
*expensive-looking ink pen*
*little bell*
*tray with "invitations"*
*coat and hat for the butler*
*soccer uniform*
*soccer ball*
*cell phone*
*12 envelopes with "invitations" inside*

*Open on a high-backed, expensive-looking chair on one side of the stage. An Old Man is sitting in it and writing at a desk. He stops writing and rings a little bell. A butler enters, carrying a tray.*

**Butler:** *(Proper British voice)* You rang, sir?

**Old Man:** Edmond, I wish for you to deliver these six invitations personally. And please wait for the reply.

*The Butler holds out the tray. The man places very expensive-looking envelopes on the tray.*

**Butler:** Very good, sir. Will that be all?

**Old Man:** Yes, thank you.

**Butler:** Very good, sir.

*The Butler exits. (The Old Man stays in the chair, writing, during most of the drama.)*

*Albert enters in soccer uniform with ball. The Butler enters. He is in a coat and hat now.*

**Butler:** Pardon me, sir. Are you Albert?

**Albert:** Yeah, my friends call me Al. You can call me Albert. Who are you?

**Butler:** I have an invitation for you . . . sir.

**Albert:** Thanks, pal. I love parties. You're not going to be there, are you?

**Butler:** I'm sorry, sir, but I am instructed to wait for an RSVP.

**Albert:** A what?

**Butler:** That would be a reply.

**Albert:** Oh. Why didn't you say so? *(opens the letter and reads)* "You are cordially invited to attend worship service at your church . . ." Sunday, the fourteenth. That's this Sunday, right? *(to Butler)* Wait a minute. I thought this was for a party. This isn't for a party?

**Butler:** I couldn't say, sir. Does your church's worship service usually include a party?

**Albert:** Look, pal, just tell whoever sent this that I'm too busy right now. I have soccer practice on Sundays.

**Butler:** I will convey your reply to my master.

**Albert:** Yeah, you do that. And tell your "master" that invitations are supposed to be for parties.

*They exit in opposite directions. Enter Brenda, talking on a cell phone, nonstop.*

**Brenda:** So, I like said to her, "Oh my gosh, you must be like joking." And you know what she said? No. Come on. Take a guess.

*Enter the Butler, standing nearby.*

**Brenda:** *(sees Butler)* Like "duh." Of course. Hold the phone, Sophie. Like there's some fancy dude checking me out. You may need to call 9-1-1. *(to the Butler)* Can I help you?

**Butler:** I have an invitation for you, miss. *(hands it to her)*

**Brenda:** Wow! Like hand-delivered! Sophie, you'll never believe what the fancy dude did. *(notices Butler is still standing by)* Uhhh, Sophie. Let me call you back.

**Butler:** I am sorry to interrupt your conversation, miss, but I am asked by the sender to await your reply.

**Brenda:** Fanceee! *(opens invitation and reads)* "You are cordially nvited to give a tenth of your allowance to the poor." *(to Butler)* That's it?

**Butler:** Your reply, miss?

**Brenda:** Did someone put you up to this? Sophie? Come on. You can tell me.

**Butler:** I assure you the invitation is genuine.

**Brenda:** Gee! But I'm saving my money for a cell phone.

**Butler:** Pardon me if I am mistaken, miss, but it appears as though you already own a cell phone.

**Brenda:** This old thing? As if! It doesn't have Internet or call waiting, only has five different ring tones, doesn't have touch screen and, furthermore, doesn't go with my eyes.

**Butler:** I see.

**Brenda:** So, I'm very sorry, but I will have to decline this invitation.

**Butler:** Yes, miss. I am sorry to have bothered you.

*Butler exits into audience.*

**Brenda:** *(to herself, punching in a phone number)* Sophie isn't going to believe this. *(exits)*

*Butler comes up to Carrie sitting on the aisle in the audience.*

**Butler:** Excuse me, miss. Is your name Carrie?

**Carrie:** Yes. Why?

**Butler:** I have an invitation for you.

**Carrie:** Wow! You're kidding? Just like those other two people?

*(stands, takes invitation)* I was just saying how hard would it be to put aside a tenth of your allowance, and I go to church anyway. *(reads invitation)* "You are cordially invited to get along with your brother." I can't believe this. Why couldn't I just get the church one? I try, but you don't know how hard it is. He's evil. But my parents think he's an angel. He gets away with everything and he's so mean to me. Give him the invitation, not me.

**Butler:** I take it then, miss, that you are unfortunately replying in the negative.

**Carrie:** If that means it's impossible to get along with my brother— or my parents, for that matter—then yes, it means no.

**Butler:** Thank you, miss.

**Carrie:** Are you sure that I can't have the invitation to go to church?

**Butler:** Indeed, miss. You are most welcome to attend the church of your choice. And may I be so bold as to suggest that you take that time to pray for strength in dealing with your family? I am afraid, however, that I can deliver the invitations only to the individuals to whom they are addressed.

*A young couple enters the stage. The Butler sees them.*

**Butler:** I am sorry, miss. I had an older brother too. Now if you will please pardon me, I must catch up to that young couple. *(Carrie sits. Butler hurries to the stage and speaks to the couple.)* Pardon me. May I have a word with the two of you?

**Dave and Ellen:** Are you talking to us, sir?

**Butler:** I believe you are Dave and Ellen.

**Dave:** That's right.

**Ellen:** How did you know?

**Butler:** I have an invitation for each of you.

**Dave:** Wow! Cool!

**Ellen:** Oh, we don't need separate invitations. We go everywhere together.

**Butler:** Still, miss, my instructions are to give you each your own invitation.

**Ellen:** OK. *(opens and reads)* "You are cordially invited to help supervise your sister's Girl Scout troop in their downtown cleanup and recycling day next Saturday." *(to Butler)* That's odd. Did Dave get that invitation too? He can't come to a Girl Scout event, and I never go anywhere on the weekends without him. *(to Dave)* What's yours say, hon?

**Dave:** Please don't call me "hon," Ellen. You know I don't like that. *(reading)* "You are cordially invited to . . ." Uhhh . . . *(puts down the invitation)*

**Ellen:** What? What's it say?

**Dave:** Nothing. It's just some kind of ad or something.

**Ellen:** *(grabs it and reads)* "You are cordially invited to not go to any more parties where you know they serve beer." *(to Butler)* This must be a mistake! He doesn't go anywhere without . . . *(to Dave)* You've been going to Joey's parties! You said you had homework to do.

**Dave:** I did have homework to do. Then I went to the party. *(to Butler)* You look like a nice guy, sir, but Joey is a good friend of mine. I can't just blow him off.

**Butler:** I believe, sir, there is an additional part to your invitation.

**Dave:** What? *(grabs it back from Ellen and reads)* "Or, if beer is served at a party, you are cordially invited to refuse it." *(to Butler)*

9

Sir, it's really no big deal. I just have one. You know, to fit in. What can I say?

**Ellen:** I can't believe you're going to Joey's parties without me!

**Dave:** Ellen, girls aren't invited. You know that. But, really, that's beside the point. Look, sir, I'll try to keep it to half a beer.

**Butler:** You look like a nice guy too, sir, but I am afraid I will still have to take that as declining the invitation. *(to Ellen)* Perhaps, miss, you would like to do something on your own, such as . . . say . . . this Girl Scout event.

*Ellen throws down the invitation and storms off.*

**Butler:** *(reaching down to pick up invitation)* I suppose I would not be remiss in presuming that throwing down the invitation constitutes a refusal to participate in a recycling event.

**Dave:** Yeah. Take my word for it. That was a "no." Well, see you, sir. *(exits)*

**Butler:** Take care, Dave. *(looks up at lights or to back of space)* Is that you, Fred, in the light booth?

**Fred:** *(offstage, over intercom)* Yeah, it's me.

**Butler:** Is it possible, sir, that you can come down here?

**Fred:** I'm kind of busy now.

**Butler:** But the last envelope is yours.

**Fred:** For me? Are you sure? *(Butler nods yes.)* Hmmm. You mind just reading it for me?

**Butler:** I suppose that would be in order. *(opens the last invitation and reads)* "You are cordially invited to . . ." Oh, good, sir, this is an easy one! "You are cordially invited to pray for others every day." That's it, sir.

**Fred:** Every day? Without fail? Hmmmm. You know, I'm really busy these days. I have school, soccer practice, and this job. I'm tired when I get home. I just want to relax and go to sleep.

**Butler:** May I ask a question, sir?

**Fred:** What?

**Butler:** Pardon me for the following outburst. Ahem! *(Butler raises his voice.)* Haven't you been paying attention? Haven't you heard a word? Is it possible that you have learned nothing from all this? You got the easiest one by far. How long would it take? *(pretending to pray)* "Now I lay me down to sleep. I pray the Lord my soul to keep. Thank you for all my blessings. Bless Mom and Dad and Sis and Uncle Harry." That's it! Sir!

*Lights go out.*

**Butler:** Pardon me, sir. I presumed a bit too much. Please forgive me. I will relay your response to my master. *(exits)*

*The lights go up on the Old Man. The Butler enters, carrying a tray.*

**Butler:** I am afraid I am the bearer of bad news, sir.

**Old Man:** Not one of them accepted? Not even Fred?

**Butler:** No, sir. I am afraid not.

**Old Man:** *(looks angry)* Here are six letters, to go to the same six individuals. As you can see, I am not surprised in the least.

**Butler:** Very good, sir. I will deliver them immediately. *(He can exit and come back on as the five enter. Or he can just stay on, by the chair, and watch the five.)*

*Five of the six enter and line up facing the audience. Including Fred, backstage, they can read the new invitation in turn.*

**Albert:** "You are cordially invited to regret . . ."

**Brenda:** ". . . for the rest of your life . . ."

**Carrie:** ". . . your refusal to accept my kind invitation. . . ."

**Dave:** ". . . For if you had accepted it . . ."

**Ellen:** ". . . you would have become a part of . . ."

**Fred:** ". . . the Kingdom of God."

**Butler:** Remember, it was your choice to turn down the invitation.

**All:** *(looking around in surprise)* Aggggghhhhh!

**Old Man:** That will be all, Edmond.

**Butler:** Very good, sir.

# The Last Supper

## Production Notes

*This is the story of the Last Supper based upon
Matthew 26:14-35.
The story centers on the institution of Communion, Jesus' betrayal
by Judas, and his denial by Peter.
Having the scene of Judas' betrayal and Peter's declaration that he
will not betray Jesus is done intentionally to show the Last Supper's
position between the two acts of betrayal.*

*Judas, John, and Peter are the disciples called by name in this
drama. There are two unnamed disciples. (These two disciples could
be played by the actors doing John and Peter if you have a small
group, or they could be other disciples.) You can vary number of
disciples' roles to fit your group size.*

## Characters

**Speaking Roles**
Judas
High Priest (Caiaphas*)
Narrator
Jesus
John
Disciples (two or more)
A Man
Peter

**Nonspeaking Roles**
Optional:
Other Chief Priests
Servants

*Caiaphas (KAY-uh-fuhs)

## Props

*bag of "coins"
table and chairs (or floor pillows)
bread on a plate
(and two pieces of bread;
one for Jesus, and one for Judas)
Communion cup
bowl*

*Open on the Chief Priests in one corner of the stage, whispering to one another. In the farthest corner of the auditorium, Judas is running scared, hiding a bit, stopping to catch his breath, always looking behind him and around as if in fear. The Priests stay on the stage or a riser. Judas comes to the edge of the stage.*

**Judas:** Are you the High Priest Caiaphas?

**High Priest:** What do you want?

**Judas:** How much will you pay me to deliver Jesus into your hands?

*The Chief Priests look at each other, trying to disguise their surprise and smiles.*

**High Priest:** Thirty silver coins.

**Judas:** I want it now.

*The High Priest throws a bag of coins down on the floor near Judas. Judas grabs it and runs. Lights go down. All exit.*

*Lights come up on an empty stage. Narrator enters and stands to one side.*

**Narrator:** On the first day of Passover, when bread made with yeast is purged from every Jewish home, some of the disciples come to Jesus with a question.

*Jesus enters down an aisle through the audience. Jesus stands to one side of the stage. Some Disciples are with him. A couple of Disciples run from off stage and up to Jesus.*

**John:** Lord, where would you like us to make the preparations for the Passover meal?

**Jesus:** Go into the city. You will find a man there. Tell him that the Teacher says . . .

*The two Disciples go up to a Man.*

*Jesus and the two Disciples speak simultaneously.*

**Jesus:** My time is near. I will keep Passover at your house with my disciples.

**Two Disciples:** His time is near. He will keep Passover at your house with his disciples.

**Man:** Tell the Teacher that everything will be ready.

*The two Disciples exit. Servants bring out a long table and chairs and set them up. The Man watches. He may inspect things and nod or mime directions as the Servants continue. (This should not be hurried.) At last, they bring out a cup and a plate with bread. The Man walks around the table and checks things once more. He exits.*

*Lights go out and come back up with the Disciples sitting and eating and talking in groups. Jesus is sitting at the central spot at the table.*

**Jesus:** Truly I tell you . . . *(the talking stops immediately)* Truly I tell you, one of you will betray me.

**Disciples:** *(a variety of responses)* No! / Surely not! / Nobody would betray you, Lord. / Who would do such a thing? / It is impossible. / Surely, it wouldn't be me. / Not me. / It isn't me, is it, Lord?

*Judas is sitting near or across from Jesus. During the commotion, Judas and Jesus dip their bread into a bowl at the same time.*

**Jesus:** It is the one who has dipped his hand into the bowl with me.

**Disciples:** Who? / Who did that? / Do you mean just now? / Who was it? / Who dipped his hand?

**Jesus:** The Son of Man goes as it is written of him. But woe to the one by whom the Son of Man is betrayed. It would be better if he had never been born.

**Judas:** Surely it is not I, Lord?

**Jesus:** You have said so.

*Judas stares at him, shakes his head, and exits.*

**Disciples:** How could he do such a thing? / Lord, are you sure? / I always knew it. / Of course, Judas. / I never liked him. / Me neither. / Surely nobody would betray Jesus. / Maybe he's just angry.

**Jesus:** *(rising)* Father, bless this bread we are about to eat.

**Disciples:** Amen.

**Jesus:** Take and eat this bread. This is my body.

*Each take a piece of bread as it is passed.*

**Jesus:** *(holding up the cup)* Father, bless this wine we are about to drink.

**Disciples:** Amen.

**Jesus:** Drink from it, all of you. This is my blood of the new covenant, which is poured out for many for the forgiveness of sins. I tell you, I will never again drink of this fruit of the vine until that day when I drink it new with you in my Father's kingdom.

**Disciples:** New covenant? / What's that mean? / What does he mean? / Not drink it again until when? / I don't understand. / What's going on? / Is Jesus going somewhere? / Some land we don't know about?

**Jesus:** I think we should end this feast with music, don't you?

**Narrator:** Jesus and the disciples end the Passover feast with a hymn. When they finish, they leave and go out to the Mount of Olives.

*Lights dim.*

**Jesus:** (*offstage*) Tonight, all of you will desert me. It is written, "God will smite the shepherd and the flock will be scattered." But after I have been raised up, I will go to Galilee and meet you there.

*Lights come up low on the opposite side of stage from where the High Priests were at the beginning. Jesus enters, followed by Peter. Peter stops Jesus.*

**Peter:** Even if everyone else deserts you, Lord, I would never do that.

**Jesus:** The truth is, Peter, that this very night, before the cock crows at dawn, you will deny me three times.

**Peter:** Never, Lord! I would die first!

*Jesus looks at him sadly, pats him gently on the shoulder, then turns and exits. After a moment, Peter, head bowed, follows.*

# Camp TLC

## Production Notes

*This drama is done in a contemporary camp setting. The number of campers can be adjusted up or down. This drama is a fun way to explore how Christians should be known for the way they live.*

## Characters

### Speaking Roles
Counselor (Michael)
Camper #1
Camper #2
Camper #3
Camper #4
Camper #5
Camper #6
Camper #7
Camper #8
(After first introduction each camper is designated only by number.)
Nathan
Gabe

### Nonspeaking Roles
Optional:
as many campers as you want

## Props
*TLC T-shirts for everyone*

*The Campers enter. They have T-shirts with "Camp TLC" on them. An offstage voice directs them.*

**Counselor:** *(offstage)* All right, recruits. That's right. Step forward please. Line up. Thank you. Welcome to Camp TLC. We'll be right with you.

**Camper #1:** Wow! Camp TLC! Sounds like fun, huh?

**Camper #2:** Well, some friends of mine who have been here seem to be better people for it. Happier too. It looks hard though.

**Camper #3:** My brother came back from it three years ago. He hasn't been the same since.

**#1:** Wow! Really?

**#3:** Yeah. He never picks on me anymore.

**#2:** Did he pick on you before?

**#3:** Yeah. All the time. Now he says things like, "Can I get you something while I'm up?" and "Hey, bro. You want anything from the store? My treat."

**#2:** Whoa! Creepy!

**#3:** You said it.

**Counselor:** Good morning, new Christians.

*Nobody answers.*

**Counselor:** I'm talking to you guys. Good morning, new Christians.

**Everyone:** Good morning, sir.

**Counselor:** You don't have to call me "sir." You may call me Michael. Welcome to Camp TLC.

**Camper #4:** Excuse me, sir. Michael, I mean. What does TLC stand for?

**Counselor:** Thank you for asking. It stands for Training to Live (or Love) like a Christian.

**Camper #5:** I thought it stood for Tender Loving Care.

**Counselor:** No. That's part of it, of course. But this is a training camp. Designed to teach you to spot a Christian. That's very important these days. But more important, it's designed to teach you to spot the Christian in yourself, so that you can learn to live (and love) like a Christian. Be seated and we will start with the first lesson.

*The campers can sit on the stage to one side, partially facing the audience. Nathan and Gabe enter to center stage.*

**Counselor:** My fellow counselors, Nathan and Gabe, will demonstrate.

**Nathan:** *(to Gabe)* Hello. I'm the new kid. Do you know where Room 357 is?

**Gabe:** No.

**Nathan:** Oh. Well, do you know where the science labs are?

**Gabe:** Look. No offense, but I just don't talk to the new kids, OK?

**Counselor:** Stop! *(to campers)* OK. So is Gabe acting like a Christian?

**#4:** Well, the guy *is* a new guy.

**#3:** And at least Gabe didn't shove him into a locker.

**Counselor:** So, you think he was being a Christian, just ignoring him?

**#5:** No, the Christian shows the new guy around.

**Camper #6:** Yeah. He should make him feel welcome. Introduce him to his friends.

**Counselor:** Good job, guys! In the old days, a Christian would have put the guy up and given him food.

**Camper #7:** What if the guy turns out to be a jerk?

**Camper #8:** Yeah. Or even a bully?

**Counselor:** Good question. OK, let's talk about our quote-unquote "enemies," like bullies and mean people. What do we do with them?

**#8:** Give them the ole one-two?

**#7:** Yeah! Punch 'em in the nose.

**#6:** Excu-u-se me. But I don't think Christ wants us punching anyone in the nose.

**Counselor:** Right you are, Number Six. The Lord commands us to turn the other cheek. That means having the courage to walk away.

**#3:** What if they play mean tricks on us?

**#1:** Or steal something from us?

**#8:** Or bang a locker on our hand? or trip us in front of girls? or give us a wedgie? or . . .

**#5:** Yeah. What if they challenge us and lots of people are watching? If we walk away, we'll look like cowards.

**Counselor:** No. It takes a lot more courage to just ignore bullies or walk away. And what do you do when your friends are being mean? Does the Christian punch his friend in the nose? Watch Gabe and Nathan.

**Gabe:** Nathan, how are you doing?

**Nathan:** Hey, Gabe. How ya been?

**Gabe:** Hey, I learned a trick from my brother. Hey, what's that? *(pointing up)*

**Nathan:** What? Where? *(As he looks up, Gabe pretends to poke him in the throat.)* Ow! That hurt.

**Gabe:** Hey, Nathan, is that something on your shirt?

**Nathan:** What? Where? *(He looks down to where Gabe is pointing and Gabe raises his finger and pretends to poke him in the nose.)* Ow!

**Counselor:** So, should Nathan knock his friend's block off? Punch his lights out? Gabe hurt him twice, after all.

**All:** No!

**Counselor:** No. Why not?

**#1:** Because—like you said—it's not the Christian thing to do.

**Counselor:** So, does Nathan just let him be mean to him?

**#3:** Well, he could tell Gabe how he feels.

**Counselor:** Exactly.

**Nathan:** Gabe, I didn't like those tricks. My throat still hurts. I won't hang out with you anymore if you keep it up.

**Gabe:** Sorry, Nathan. I shouldn't have done them. Come to think of it, I didn't like it when my brother did them to me. You OK?

**Nathan:** Yeah. That's OK. Thanks for apologizing.

**Counselor:** Christians don't believe in revenge, do we?

**#5:** But, Michael, it's hard sometimes to forgive people when you're still hurting.

**Counselor:** Sure it is. But it gets easier every time. Here. We'll practice some easier stuff. Up here. Pair off. Nathan and Gabe will help you in these next little exercises.

*The campers pair off. Nathan and Gabe whisper something to the different pairs.*

**#1 and #2:** We're looking for the good in each other.

**#1:** Oh, that's a nice tan you have.

**#2:** Thank you. Your teeth are quite straight.

**Counselor:** Not bad. Practice looking for the good in a little more important things though. Next.

**#3:** How are you doing?

**#4:** I'm sad. My cat just died.

**#3:** Oh, that's sad. I know you were attached to that cat, even though it really had a lot of fleas.

**Counselor:** *(sighs)* OK. When showing empathy, though, try to say all nice things.

**#3:** I've got it. *(to #4)* I heard your project won at the science fair. That's great. You really deserve it. I know you really worked hard.

**#4:** Yes. Thanks, I did. I saw your project. It was awesome. You deserve an award too.

**Counselor:** Very good. Next.

**#5:** What's wrong?

**#6:** Oh, I'm fine. Well, my toes hurt a little where I stubbed them last night, and my parents have taken away my text-messaging privileges, and Mrs. Cowen hates me, and coach says I need to work harder to make first string—but I'm feeling better, and I deserve the punishment, and I just need to work harder in Mrs. Cowen's class and try harder for coach. Hey! Thanks for asking.

**Counselor:** Not bad. A Christian must "suffer with patience" or, put another way, keep a positive attitude! Although, it really isn't necessary to explain all your problems in great detail. Great job, especially for the first day! OK, campers. There's lots more. We'll break for lunch. Afterward, I want you to pair off and practice showing empathy. We'll meet back here in an hour.

*The campers all rush offstage yelling.*

**Gabe:** Not bad for Day One, I'd say. Not bad at all.

**Nathan:** A week of TLC and they'll be like they were born again.

**Counselor:** Well, they won't be punching anyone in the nose or ignoring the new kid at least.

**Gabe:** Hey, like you said, keep a positive attitude.

**Counselor:** Oh. Thank you so much for reminding me, Gabe.

**Nathan:** Let's get some lunch.

*They laugh and pat each other on the back and exit.*

# Plan B

## Production Notes

*This modern drama is about the necessity of everyone in the family of God using the gifts given by the Holy Spirit to accomplish good. This story is a good accompaniment to any Bible story connected to the teaching that no task is too small to help further the kingdom of God.*

*The speaking parts for this drama can be expanded in number by having unnamed Servers speak some of the lines designated as "All" or "The Others," where many are meant to be speaking at the same time.*

## Characters

### Speaking Roles
Mrs. Charmichael (Mrs. C)
Megan
Terry
Dave
Phil
Carol
Donna

### Nonspeaking Roles
Optional:
Servers
Homeless People

## Props

*tablecloths*
*tables*
*chairs*
*dishes, cups, and pitchers*
*papers*
*a watch*
*cell phones*
*a Bible*
*loaf of bread*

*A soup kitchen setup. A buffet line with kids (Megan, Terry, Dave, Donna) serving. Adults, or kids dressed up as adults, are in line getting food. Some of them are at a table already eating. Carol and Phil are pouring drinks for the people at the table.*

*On the other side of the stage from the buffet line, with different lighting, is a table full of papers. This is the planning table.*

*Mrs. Charmichael enters. Goes to Megan behind the buffet line.*

**Mrs. Charmichael:** Megan, this is terrific. You guys did a great job planning this soup kitchen.

**Megan:** Thanks, Mrs. Charmichael. Well, we had all these grand plans, you know. Roasted turkey with all the trimmings. It turned into just sandwiches and canned soup.

**Terry:** And potato salad and chips!

**Dave:** And ice cream!

**Megan:** Right. And a few other things. But we got it together finally.

**Mrs. C:** Oh? Did you have a tough time planning it?

**Megan:** You can say that again.

*Lights change to planning table. Mrs. C and Megan exit. Phil goes to table and sits down and is reading the Bible. Megan enters, frazzled. The Homeless People either freeze or go sit down.*

**Megan:** Sorry I'm late, Phil. Are you the only one here?

**Phil:** Hi, Megan. Yep. Well, Carol was here but she forgot the ice. She'll be right back.

**Megan:** I can't believe this. The soup kitchen is in a couple of hours. There's no food, no drinks, and no people to help.

**Phil:** Well, there's drinks. I brought the lemonade.

**Megan:** Great! We'll serve them lemonade in bowls.

**Phil:** Relax, Megan. Look! There's Dave and Terry now.

*Dave and Terry enter.*

**Dave:** Hey, Meg. Whassup! Sorry we're late.

**Megan:** Aren't you forgetting something?

**Terry:** Yeah, Dave. *(to Megan, bowing)* He means we're very sorry we're late.

**Megan:** You guys! Come on! What about the food?

**Dave:** No thanks. I'm not hungry.

**Terry:** Uh oh. I seem to recall I may have signed up to bring something.

**Dave:** Yeah, Terry. You're supposed to bring potato chips and salad. How could you forget that?

**Terry:** Actually, it was potato salad and chips—at least I think it was—and what about you? The words "ice cream" mean anything to you?

**Dave:** Weren't you going to e-mail me a reminder, Megan?

*Carol enters.*

**Carol:** Sorry I'm late. I had to go home to get ice.

**Dave:** See, even Carol forgot something.

**Terry:** Yeah, and she's a lot smarter than Dave. *(Dave looks at him.)* Well, of course she is, Dave. Carol's even smarter than me.

*Donna enters.*

**Donna:** Hi, guys. Sorry I'm late.

**Megan**: Please tell me you didn't forget the turkey and trimmings, Donna.

**Donna:** Forget? No, I've called every restaurant in town. Megan, nobody wants to donate a whole turkey—cooked. I told you.

**Dave:** Plus all the trimmings.

**Megan:** So, basically, what you're saying is that nobody has accomplished any of their tasks and the soup kitchen is two hours (*checks her watch*)—no, ninety minutes—from now, and we have nothing. Nothing at all!

**The Others:** *(all at the same time and getting louder)* Hey. We're busy. / You're asking a lot. / Nobody's got time for all this. / I've tried. / Didn't you get my e-mail? I updated you. / I sent you an e-mail asking if you had talked to anyone about drinks. / Drinks are easy. Anyone can get drinks. / I can't believe this. / Everyone had a set of tasks and nobody's done anything. / There was never enough time. I told you that. / No you didn't. / Of course I did. Every meeting we've had. / That's the problem. Too many meetings. / Obviously that's not the only problem.

*Phil has been sitting silently through all this, just watching. He thumbs through his Bible to the right page. Stands up.*

**Phil:** *(clearing throat)* Ahem!

*The others immediately stop their loud arguing and look up questioningly at Phil.*

**Phil:** *(too quietly)* I was thinking that a passage from Galatians—

**Dave:** *(respectfully)* Excuse me, Phil. What did you say?

28

**Phil:** Suggestion. I think that this passage from Paul's letter to the Galatians, called fruit of the Spirit, will help get us on the right course.

**All:** OK. / Sounds good. / Great. / Read on. / Can't hurt. / We need something.

**Phil:** It's from chapter 5, verse 22. When the Holy Spirit controls our lives, this kind of fruit is in us: *(reading)* "love, joy, peace, patience, kindness, generosity, faithfulness, gentleness, and self-control."

*A moment of silence while everyone thinks about this. Phil sits down.*

**Megan:** Thank you, Phil.

**Carol:** You do get to the heart of the matter, Phil. We were all happy and cheerful when we first decided to do the soup kitchen. I guess we've lost a lot of that.

**Megan:** OK. Well . . . we can get that back. I realize I haven't been very patient. Now, though, I see that maybe we need a Plan B. Would sandwiches be OK with everyone?

**Donna:** Great. *(pulling out her cell phone)* I'll ask my Mom to bring some sandwich stuff from home.

**Dave:** I think there's some ice cream in the freezer left over from youth group. I'll check. *(exits)*

**Terry:** And the church pantry always has condiments.

**Phil:** I'll check to make sure. There's usually bread too. *(exits to pantry)*

**Carol:** *(pulls out cell phone)* Let me see if my brother can pick up some stuff from the deli.

**Terry:** Thanks, Carol. *(to nobody in particular)* See, I told you she was smart.

**Donna:** *(on the phone)* My mom says she'll swing by the grocery store too, to pick up stuff. Phil, do we need bread?

**Phil:** *(enters, carrying a loaf)* Yes, we could probably use an extra loaf. But there's plenty of condiments. I'll chip in for meats and stuff.

**The Others:** Yeah. / I can pay. / Me too. / My folks will contribute. / I'll contribute myself.

**Dave:** *(enters)* We'll probably need an extra gallon of ice cream too. I'll pay for that. That was my responsibility, after all.

**Megan:** Thanks, Dave.

**Carol:** *(on phone)* My brother can pick up the potato salad and chips from the deli. He'll be here in ten minutes.

**Megan:** Great! Now we're talking. I'll get the tablecloths.

**Phil:** We'll set up the tables and chairs.

**Carol:** And you can count on me to help make the sandwiches.

**Megan:** Awesome. It'll be fun. We can set up a sandwich assembly line.

*The lights start to cross-fade back to the soup kitchen. The kids continue the dialogue as they take their places back where they were at the beginning.*

**Dave:** I'll get bowls and start dishing out the ice cream.

**Megan:** It seems like we're forgetting something . . .

**Donna:** *(still on the phone)* The drinks, the dessert. We've already got all the plates . . .

**Phil:** I know what we forgot.

**Dave:** Oh yeah . . .

**Everyone:** THE SOUP!!!!

*They all say this at once and laugh uproariously. By this time, Mrs. C has entered and is standing where she was at the beginning.*

**Mrs. C:** That's funny. Well, I'm glad you remembered the soup for the soup kitchen.

**Terry:** Yeah. Otherwise, we wouldn't know what to call it.

**Mrs. C:** I'm proud of you guys. You started over and got it together. You all pitched in and did a very valuable thing.

**Dave:** Yeah, maybe instead of Plan B, we should call it Plan C.

**Mrs. C:** Why is that, Dave?

**Dave:** You know. C. For Christian. *(turns to one of the tables)* Who wants ice cream? Great. Here you go. Here, have some more. . . .

*(Improvise into a fade out as they all continue to help the people.)*

# This Is Your Life, Paul!

## Production Notes

*This drama uses the format of an old television show called "This Is Your Life!" to give a shortened overview of Paul's life and the people whose lives he affected.*

*You can add "Audience Members" if you need more parts. Some actors may play more than one character if there are too few actors.*

*Although many spots call for "hugging," tweens don't really like to hug. Instead, characters could pat each other on the back or shake hands.*

## Characters

### Speaking Roles
Announcer
Host (Edward Ralphs)
Paul
Ananias*
Barnabas
Silas
Timothy
Lydia
Priscilla
Chloe*
Eutychus*
Philemon*
Agrippa*
Julius

### Nonspeaking Roles
Aquila*
Optional: Audience Members


*Ananias (an-uh-NIGH-uhs)
Chloe (KLOH-ee)
Eutychus (YOO-tuh-kuhs)
Philemon (fi-LEE-muhn)
Agrippa (uh-GRIP-uh)
Aquila (AK-wi-luh)

## Props

*chair*
*stool*
*suit for Host*
*"This Is Your Life!" oversized book*
*Optional: screen for actors to stand behind*
*CD and CD player*

*Chair sits center stage facing audience. Host's stool is next to it. The testimonial guests speak into a mike either offstage or behind a screen where the audience can see them but Paul can't. As the lights come up, "game show" music is playing.*

**Announcer:** Ladies and gentlemen, welcome to This is Your Life! Now put your hands together for our host, Edward Ralphs.

*Host enters, dressed in suit, carrying a book that says "This Is Your Life!" He bows to audience.*

**Host:** Thank you, everybody, and welcome to our show. It's going to be one of our best ever today, I'm sure, because we are so lucky to have such an honored guest.

This person was once called Saul, but most of us know him by a different name. This man is responsible for much of the New Testament and, for that matter, much of the spread of Christianity itself. Please welcome the apostle, the extraordinary leader . . . ladies and gentlemen, I present Paul of Tarsus. Paul, this is your life!

*Audience applauds. Paul enters. Bows ever so slightly. Shakes the Host's hand. Tries humbly to quell the applause. Host shows him to his chair. They both sit.*

**Paul:** Thank you, Edward. Thank you, all. I don't deserve that.

**Host:** I think most of us would disagree with you on that, Paul. Does all that applause make you a bit uncomfortable?

**Paul:** I'm afraid so. They told me I was coming in to tape part of a documentary on Easter.

**Host:** *(chuckles)* Yes. We like to surprise our guests, and you're in for quite a few surprises. We've brought in people from all over the Mediterranean who have been part of your life to honor you here tonight.

**Paul:** Oh, please. This is too much.

**Host:** Well, Paul, your life has been exemplary like few others. But you weren't always so saintly. As a young man and a leading Pharisee, you felt it was your job to destroy Christianity, didn't you? But then one day as you were traveling to Damascus, something happened.

**Paul:** Yes. Christ spoke to me.

**Host:** And what did he say?

**Paul:** Well, he said he was Jesus, and that I was persecuting him by persecuting his followers.

**Host:** And you were struck blind, weren't you? And led to Damascus by your fellow travelers.

**Ananias:** *(offstage)* You can imagine when the Lord told me to go find Paul of Tarsus in Damascus, I was terrified. I thought I too might be arrested and executed.

**Paul:** Ananias?!

*Ananias enters and hugs Paul.*

**Host:** That's right. Ananias, the man who baptized Paul. So, Ananias, you found Paul and he was blind?

**Ananias:** Yes. I laid my hands on him and—just like that, he could see. Then I baptized him. And I tell you something. Paul was filled with the Holy Spirit from the very beginning. His understanding of Christ was almost immediate.

**Paul:** Ananias helped me to see in more ways than one.

**Host:** That's great. Well, thank you so much for coming to be a part of Paul's life tonight, Ananias. We'll see you at the end of the show.

**Ananias:** My pleasure. *(He exits. Paul sits.)*

**Host:** Despite the fact that you were a fervent preacher of the gospel, when you went to Jerusalem to meet with the disciples, they were afraid of you.

**Barnabas:** *(offstage)* The twelve thought that Paul was up to his same old tricks. So I went with him and introduced him to them and assured them of Paul's conversion.

*Barnabas enters and hugs Paul.*

**Host:** Your old traveling buddy, Barnabas, who went with you on your first missionary journey. So, Barnabas, you guys ran into some difficulties in many places, didn't you?

**Barnabas:** Practically every place, Edward. But we expected that. The authorities, the wealthy sometimes, the leaders of the synagogues didn't like what we had to say.

**Paul:** But the Lord protected us and saved us from certain death on many occasions.

**Host:** Tell us what happened in Lystra.

**Barnabas:** That's a funny story. There was this crippled man, and Paul cured him. The people all around who saw this thought we were gods in human form!

**Paul:** I was a bit peeved actually. They thought I was just Hermes, the messenger of the gods, while Barnabas, here, got to be Zeus, the head god.

**Barnabas:** Actually, the whole thing was very upsetting at the time.

**Host:** I'll bet. So, after a lot of time together, the two of you didn't exactly separate on the best of terms.

**Paul:** Yes, we disagreed about whether to take Barnabas's cousin, John Mark, with us on a journey.

**Barnabas:** I think it was all for the best actually. We were able to spread the word in many more places. As Paul says in one of his letters to the Corinthians, we're all on the same team.

**Host:** Indeed. Another traveling companion of Paul, this man joined you on your second missionary journey.

**Silas:** *(offstage)* Talk about no good deed goes unpunished. In Philippi, Paul cast a demon out of a slave girl. Her master was very angry because he could no longer make money from the girl, so he had us flogged and put into prison.

*Silas enters and joins Barnabas and Paul. Much hugging.*

**Host:** So you two were thrown into prison?

**Paul:** Yes, but then an earthquake came and flung open all the prison doors.

**Silas:** But, of course, Paul didn't want to escape because the jailer would get in trouble. Instead, Paul converted the jailer and all his family. Meanwhile, the Philippian officials were begging us to leave because they didn't want to get into trouble.

**Host:** We have yet another favorite traveling companion . . . your old friend, Timothy!

*Timothy enters. Hugs all around.*

**Host:** Timothy, you were with Paul when he wrote some of his most important letters, weren't you?

**Timothy:** Yes. I took a lot of dictation from this man, believe me. Romans. Corinthians. Philippians.

**Paul:** And if he wasn't with me traveling, he was carrying my letters to all parts of the world.

**Host:** Well, gentlemen, thank you so much for coming and telling us about such exciting parts of Paul's life. *(They exit. Paul sits.)* We'll bring everyone back, but now another side. Though it was quite radical at the time, you had many ladies who were important in your ministry.

**Lydia:** *(offstage)* Most people would have left town as soon as they were released from jail, but Paul couldn't resist the chance to give one more sermon. He came to my house and preached to the converted of Philippi before leaving town.

**Paul:** Oh, Lydia. Lydia.

*She enters and they hug.*

**Host:** Lydia, you were the head of a household and a wealthy merchant? That was rare for a woman, wasn't it?

**Paul:** Well, Lydia is a rare woman. She always opened her house to any Christian.

**Lydia:** The proudest day of my life was when my entire household was baptized by Paul.

**Host:** Well, let's hear from another "rare woman."

**Priscilla:** *(offstage)* My husband and I were devastated when the emperor Claudius kicked us out of Rome. But it was really the best thing that ever happened to us. Otherwise, we may never have met Paul.

*Priscilla and Aquila enter. Hugs.*

**Host:** Priscilla and her husband, Aquila. You two have something very unique in common with Paul, besides Christ, don't you?

**Priscilla:** Yes, Edward. We are all tentmakers. We worked together in Corinth, making both tents and Christians.

**Host:** And speaking of Corinth, we have another surprise guest from that magnificent city. Here's your friend and servant in Christ, Chloe.

**Everyone:** Chloe!

*They hug.*

**Host:** Is it true, Chloe, that you are the inspiration for Paul's first letter to Corinth, certainly one of his most moving?

**Chloe:** Well, Edward, I think God is the inspiration for all of Paul's letters. But, yes, I was very worried about all of the people who were tearing the Corinthian community apart and I managed to get a letter to Paul about my concerns.

**Paul:** Chloe is just being modest. The church at Corinth might have split into any number of factions without her leadership.

**Host:** Now this was a really radical idea at the time, wasn't it— having women play important roles in churches?

**Paul:** Yes it was. Thank you for asking, Edward. Women weren't even counted as citizens. I'd say it's still a radical idea in some parts of the world.

**Host:** *(chuckles)* I see you haven't lost any of that fire, Paul. Well, let's say goodbye to these lovely church leaders for now. Thank you, ladies.

*A few quick hugs. Aquila and ladies exit.*

**Host:** Our next guest literally owes his life to Paul, in a rather special way.

**Eutychus:** *(offstage)* One night around midnight, after several hours of listening to Paul speak at a meeting, I fell asleep. That wouldn't have been so bad, but I was sitting in a windowsill and I fell three stories to the ground.

**Host:** Ladies and gentlemen, from Troas, Turkey, please welcome Eutychus, whose name aptly means "lucky."

*Eutychus enters and before Paul can hug him, he bows to Paul.*

**Eutychus:** I owe this man my life. He rushed down three flights and was the first to grab me. I don't care what anyone says. I was dead. I saw my life pass before me, and Paul brought me back to life.

**Paul:** Well, God brought you back. I just prayed real hard.

**Eutychus:** I never ever fell asleep during a meeting again. And of course, I gave up sitting on windowsills.

*Eutychus exits.*

**Host:** Thank you, Eutychus. That's a great story. There's another letter with a great story, and here to tell it is your longtime friend, Philemon.

**Paul:** Philemon! Wow!

*Philemon, a big, in-charge executive type enters. Pats Paul on the back.*

**Philemon:** This guy! I want to tell you, this guy can write! One day a runaway slave of mine named Onesimus returns out of the clear blue. I tell you, I was more surprised than angry, because I figured he was long gone. Anyway, he is carrying this letter and lo and behold it's from Paul, and he's asking me to free Onesimus. And the letter is so brilliant and diplomatic that there is no way that anyone could refuse it.

**Host:** So, you freed Onesimus?

**Philemon:** Are you kidding? I would have even if I didn't know Paul. But I figure, this is the right-hand man of Jesus Christ asking me a personal favor.

**Host:** Indeed, Paul's writing skills were renowned. He was also noted for stirring up people. Paul, when you were arrested for heresy, you were brought before this man, King Agrippa!

*Agrippa enters. Paul bows but Philemon doesn't.*

**Agrippa:** Paul, of all the speeches that were ever made before me, yours was the finest I ever heard.

**Host:** So, King Agrippa, you cleared him of the charges?

**Agrippa:** Yes, I did. But Paul insisted on a Roman trial, and as a Roman citizen he had that right. If he hadn't appealed to Caesar, he would have been set free.

**Host:** Well, thank you for coming, Your Highness.

**Agrippa:** Not at all. Thank you for asking me.

*Agrippa and Philemon exit.*

**Host:** After the trial before Agrippa, you set sail for Rome; but it was very late in the season for sailing, which was very risky. Your ship got caught in a storm and you landed on the Island of Malta.

**Julius:** *(offstage)* After we landed, Paul was gathering wood for a fire. A poisonous snake bit him. Everyone thought he was a goner. Not me, though. I knew he would survive. And he did, of course, without even a scar.

**Paul:** Julius, the Imperial Guard!

**Host:** That's right! The officer who watched over you all the way to Rome.

*Julius comes out and salutes Paul, then hugs him.*

**Host:** So, Julius, you witnessed a miracle with the snake bite?

**Julius:** I spent many months with this man, and I saw so many miracles that the snake was just one more. You know, he saved everyone's life on the boat. Some of the sailors wanted to abandon it, but Paul told them to stay. They knew Paul's God was the only God—and they listened to Paul and they all survived.

*All of the others return to the stage and stand behind Paul, who is also standing and getting more and more teary eyed.*

**Host:** Like all of these stories today, that is a testament to the overwhelming power of Paul's faith. Paul, you did make it to Rome, where you were able to write many more letters before you died. And these letters have guided millions of Christians through 2,000 years in all kinds of ways.

So, Paul of Tarsus, we thank God for you and all you have done in Christ's name. And we have only one more thing to say: Paul. . .

**All:** This is your life!

*Applause by all the people on stage and the audience. After the Host shakes his hand and hugs him, a few others come forward to give him hugs again: Timothy, Chloe, Priscilla, and maybe a couple of others.*

# A Family's Story

## Production Notes

*This drama is based on the Book of Ruth. It tells the story of faithful Ruth who refuses to leave her mother-in-law. It also tells the story of Ruth and Boaz, the parents of King David's ancestor, Obed.*

*Most parts are very small and actors could easily combine roles.*

## Characters

### Speaking Roles
Narrator
Elimelech*
First Son
Orpah*
Second Son
Naomi
Ruth
Boaz
Foreman
Cousin
Head Witness
Witnesses

### Nonspeaking Roles
Optional:
Reapers
Audience Members
Servants


*Elimelech (i-LIM-uh-lek)
Orpah (OR-puh)

## Props

*picnic blanket and basket*
*large basket for "gleaning"*
*pair of sandals for the Cousin*
*optional: rice, birdseed, or flower petals for throwing*

*As Narrator says their names, the characters enter and stand facing the audience at stage left.*

**Narrator:** In the days when the judges ruled in Israel, there was a man from Bethlehem named Elimelech. He had a wife named Naomi, and two sons. One day, Elimelech decides to abandon his land and move with his family to a nearby country, called Moab.

*The family gathers all their stuff and moves to the other side of the stage, right. They plop their stuff down.*

**Narrator:** While in Moab, Elimelech dies.

**Elimelech:** *(to Narrator)* Already? That's a pretty small part.

**Narrator:** Sorry. It is written.

*Elimelech shrugs and falls down "dead." The sons carry him off. Naomi cries.*

**Narrator:** Not long after that, the two sons marry girls from Moab. The first one marries a girl named Orpah.

*First son returns with Orpah. Naomi throws rice.*

**First Son:** *(confused)* I love your TV show.

**Orpah:** Uhh, that's not me. That's Oprah. My name's Orpah.

**First Son:** Oh. *(a pause)* I love your magazine.

**Orpah:** That's not me either. My name's *ORPAH*!

**First Son:** Oh.

**Narrator:** The second son marries a beautiful woman named Ruth.

*Second son enters with Ruth. The others throw rice.*

**Narrator:** Soon, though, both sons die too.

**Sons:** *(to Narrator)* What?!

**Narrator:** Sorry. It is written.

**Second Son:** Oh well. At least I get this one line. *(exits)*

**First Son:** Bye, Oprah!

**Orpah:** That's Orpah!

**First Son:** I love your book list. *(exits)*

**Naomi:** I must go home to Israel. And you two must return to the houses of your parents so they can take care of you.

**Orpah:** It hurts me to part, especially because you are a great mother-in-law. But I think you're right. I don't wish to be so far from my family. Goodbye, Naomi. Goodbye, Ruth.

*They hug. Orpah exits.*

**Naomi:** She's a sweet girl, but why would any parent name their child after a whale?! Isn't that cruel? Well, goodbye, Ruth.

**Ruth:** Goodbye, Naomi.

*They hug, but Ruth just follows Naomi closely.*

**Naomi:** Goodbye, Ruth.

*Ruth stays right by Naomi as she walks away.*

**Naomi:** I don't know about Moab, Ruth, but in Israel, when you say goodbye, that usually means you go off in separate directions.

**Ruth:** Yes, I know, Naomi. But I just can't leave you. You're such a great mother-in-law. I'm closer to you than my own mother. I want to go where you go. *(They take a few steps.)* I want to live where you live. *(They take a few more steps.)* I can't help it. I want your people to be my people and your God to be my God. Where you die, I want—

**Naomi:** OK, Ruth. I get the picture. You're coming back to Bethlehem. Let's not talk about dying, though, OK? I think we're pretty safe, though. We're the only characters left besides the Narrator.

*They gather up some possessions and walk back to the other side of the stage.*

**Narrator:** When the women return to Bethlehem, it is the beginning of the barley harvest. Owners of the fields are commanded by law to leave part of the barley for the poor, widows, and foreigners to pick up so they will not starve.

**Ruth:** Naomi, did you hear that? The poor, the widows, and the foreigners? I'm all three. I think I'll go gather up some barley.

**Naomi:** That would be very kind of you, Ruth. After that trip, I'm very tired. I have a wealthy relative who owns some barley fields. I hear he is very kind. Go glean in one of his fields.

*Naomi exits. The Reapers enter and mime cutting barley. The Foreman stands watching them and taking notes. Ruth kneels down and mimes picking up pieces of barley.*

**Narrator:** As it turns out Ruth is in the barley field as the owner, Naomi's relative Boaz, arrives there.

*Boaz enters. Sees Ruth.*

**Boaz:** Excuse me, Foreman.

**Foreman:** Yes sir, boss.

**Boaz:** Who is that beautiful woman over there?

**Foreman:** That's the Moab girl, sir, come back with Naomi. She's been here all morning, picking up the grains dropped by the reapers.

*Boaz goes over to her.*

**Ruth:** Thank you, Boaz.

*Servants bring out a picnic blanket and picnic basket. Ruth and Boaz sit on the blanket.*

**Boaz:** I hope you will stay in my fields and not go anywhere else. I will tell the men to be kind to you. And you can help yourself to the water.

**Ruth:** You are very kind, Boaz.

*Ruth gets up and takes a large basket to Naomi. Boaz stays seated.*

**Narrator:** Indeed, at the end of the day, Ruth returns to Naomi with a whole bushel of barley. Plus, part of her lunch.

**Naomi:** Oh, Ruth. God has indeed blessed us again. Boaz is a close relative and a kind man. You must stay in his fields. He will treat you well.

*Naomi exits. Ruth goes back to the fields, picking up grain. Boaz goes to his Foreman and talks with him and gives him instructions. The Servants remove the picnic basket and blanket from the stage.*

**Narrator:** Ruth does as Naomi instructs her and gleans the harvest of Boaz's barley and then stays on for the harvest of his wheat fields.

**Ruth:** Boaz is such a kind man. He treats me well. I can tell that he has told his workers to purposely drop part of their harvests for me to pick up.

**Boaz:** Cousin! Cousin! Just who I was looking for. How are you?

**Cousin:** Well, cousin. I hear you had a good harvest.

**Boaz:** Better than you can imagine, sir. But I have a little matter I need to discuss with you.

**Cousin:** Oh?

**Boaz:** Yes. And these men can sit as witnesses.

*Everyone gathers around. Boaz sits next to his cousin.*

**Boaz:** Naomi has decided to sell the land of our cousin, Elimelech, and you have right of first refusal.

**Cousin:** Great. Thank you, Boaz. I will buy it. I've always liked that land.

**Boaz:** Yes. I know. But I should tell you that the land comes with a little something extra.

**Cousin:** *(excited)* Oh!!

**Boaz:** Yes. You would also be acquiring the Moabite woman, Ruth, who is the widow of Elimelech's son, and her son will inherit the field.

**Cousin:** *(worried)* Oh! Oh, dear. I can't afford that, Boaz. You may take it. *(takes off one of his sandals and hands it to Boaz)* Here. You may have my sandal to seal the deal.

**Boaz:** You are my witnesses. I am acquiring the land and I am taking Ruth as my wife.

**Witnesses:** We are your witnesses.

*Naomi and Ruth rush in. Ruth hugs Boaz. Naomi throws rice.*

**Head Witness:** May the Lord make Ruth like Rachel and Leah, who together built up the house of Israel.

**Narrator:** And the Lord does just that. The son of Boaz and Ruth, Obed, is the father of Jesse. And Jesse is the father of David, and David becomes a mighty king. The end.

*NOTE: Giving of a sandal was a traditional way of confirming a deal.*